Contents

*Any words appearing in the text in bold, **like this**, are explained in the Glossary.*

What is a bush or forest fire?

Bush and forest fires are fires that burn down large areas of forest or areas we call 'bush'. Forests and bush lands are wild areas covered in plants. In forests, many trees grow closely together. In bush land there are patches of low-growing plants and fewer trees. When we say bush in this book we include areas known as the American prairies, European steppes and the Australian 'bush'.

The forests and bush lands of the world are places of great beauty. They also provide shade, food and shelter for a huge variety of plants and animals. Their plants provide us with many of the raw materials we need for building and furniture, and they also provide us with foods and medicines. One of the greatest threats to these important wild places is fire.

Forests like this also give us the **oxygen** we breathe! When plants make their food using sunlight, they release oxygen. This is an important gas in the air that we breathe to live.

Fires can spread quickly through forest and bush areas, destroying everything in their path and changing the landscape. When forest and bush fires happen near towns, there is a danger of the fires spreading to homes and other buildings.

Fires in forests and bush land can cause a lot of damage because they spread so quickly and are so hard to put out. Afterwards it can take the land a very long time to recover from a fire. Some of the trees in an ancient forest may be up to 4000 years old!

FIRE ⚡ FACTS

! Forests cover almost one-third of all the land on Earth.

! In the USA, around 5 million acres of forest burn every year.

! Around 15,000 forest fires burn in Australia every year.

A fire in bush land like this can spread fast, burning through the plants and trees that fill the area.

What causes bush and forest fires?

Fires start and spread when three vital ingredients are present — **oxygen**, **fuel** and heat. Oxygen is in the air all around us. The wood in trees makes perfect fuel. People have been using it as a fuel for centuries — to keep warm and cook food with. Heat, which is the final ingredient, can come from lightning striking the Earth. But in most cases, humans supply the heat that sparks bush and forest blazes.

FIRE ⚡ FACTS

! Fires happen regularly in forests and bush land.

! The fastest forest fires spread at speeds of up to 23 kilometres per hour. That is fast for a fire, but slow enough for people to get away.

People have known how to make fire for thousands of years. Rubbing sticks together quickly makes enough heat to cause a spark that can start a fire.

How do people start forest fires?

Most of the time, people do not mean to start forest fires. Fires can be set off in several ways. Sometimes they happen by accident, such as when sparks or **embers** from machinery, a campfire or bonfire blow onto a patch of wood shavings, dry grass or leaves. Sometimes they happen because of carelessness, such as when people drop matches or stubs of burning cigarettes to the ground or out of car windows. On some occasions, people start the fires on purpose. This is called **arson**.

In 1967 a bush fire in Hobart, Tasmania wrecked over 1400 homes and buildings. It killed 62 people and burned a vast area of forest. It began when lots of small fires that people had lit spread when a strong wind blew up.

When do bush and forest fires happen?

Large bush and forest fires usually happen when it is hot and dry. A drought is a long period of time when it does not rain. The land becomes very dry. If a drought happens when it is hot, plants take in less water. They become very dry and warm and more likely to catch fire if touched by a spark.

Wind helps spread fires. As it blows over a fire, it brings more oxygen. This makes a small fire grow bigger and wind can blow it over great distances at high speeds. Wind can also blow sparks or embers from the main fire to new places, starting new fires. In big fires, huge balls of fiery gas in the air, called fireballs, race across open land. These fireballs **ignite** trees far away from the main fire.

The new fires that start because of dropped embers or sparks are called spot fires.

Why do forest and bush plants burn so easily?

In dry conditions, fires start easily because dry grass, pine needles, dry leaves, twigs and shrubs catch fire easily. When they are alight, they heat up and dry out the trees and tree stumps around them, causing these to catch fire too. As the larger trees burn, they make a huge amount of heat. This in turn dries out other trees, which also then catch fire.

Fires also burn more quickly with certain kinds of tree. **Coniferous** trees, such as pine, contain an oily substance called resin, which burns quickly. The leaves of broad-leaved trees such as holly, evergreen oak and eucalyptus also release highly **flammable** oil in a fire.

In the Australian bush, eucalyptus trees have oily leaves and bark that comes off quickly in a fire, making them an ideal fuel for fire.

What damage do the fires cause?

Once a bush or forest fire is started, it seems to take on a life of its own. It spreads and grows quickly. It burns the trees and other plants in an area, and also threatens homes, farms, animals and people nearby.

Do forest fires hurt people?

Lots of people like to live in or near **wilderness** areas like forests and bush land. They also like to visit these places to camp, walk or watch wildlife. Sometimes, large forest fires trap people and they may be injured or killed by the flames or by falling trees. Sometimes large forest fires burn for days or weeks, creating so much smoke that it harms people. A large number of fire injuries happen when people breathe in smoke.

Forest and bush fires can hurt people, but people are usually able to walk or drive away from danger. This man is taking his pet birds to a safe place.

Why is smoke dangerous?

Smoke is produced when water and some of the chemicals inside plants and trees heat up in a fire and evaporate. This means that the water and chemicals turn into vapour – gas in the air. Smoke also contains tiny bits of **ash**, the powdered remains of wood after it is burnt. When people breathe smoke into their lungs the chemicals and ash affect their breathing. If smoke fills their lungs it can **suffocate** them.

Other problems

Forest fires can cause other problems. Burning trees may fall onto major roads, cutting off important routes. They may also block or burn bridges and telephone lines. If the fires are near towns or cities, they can spread to the buildings. Usually, **firefighters** manage to keep blazes away from places where many people live.

Firefighters usually wear special masks to prevent them from breathing in too much damaging smoke.

What happens to forest and bush animals?

Some forest animals die in major forest or bush fires. Some may be badly burned, but most suffocate because of smoke fumes. When fires happen in areas where animals are **endangered**, there is a risk that particular types of animal may be lost forever. Most animals, though, are very good at escaping fire.

Birds can usually fly away. However, fire is more dangerous for them if it happens in the nesting season, when their eggs or young are in nests. Large mammals, such as deer and wolves, usually have time to walk or run away from fire. Also, most fires leave some patches of ground untouched, so some animals escape into these. Small mammals and insects that cannot fly hide in burrows underground.

This Indian elephant is on the move to avoid the approaching flames and smoke it has spotted.

Black Christmas in Australia, 2001

In 2001, at Christmas time – which is early summer in south-east Australia – the weather was very hot and plants in the bush were dry. Lightning strikes caused some fires and a few more were started by **arson**. These small fires were then whipped up by strong winds and became vast bush fires. The flames spread throughout the state of New South Wales, coming dangerously close to the coast, where many people live. **Firefighters** struggled to stop them. They just managed to keep them from spreading into Sydney, the country's largest city. Finally, on 7 January 2002, heavy rain fell, putting out many of the fires. By then, hundreds of thousands of acres of forest had been destroyed and around 200 homes had been burnt.

Fifteen-year-old Renee said that the smoke from fires burning 20 minutes away still made her eyes water: *'It's all you can smell when you step outside,'* she said. *'The smoke is unbelievable.'*

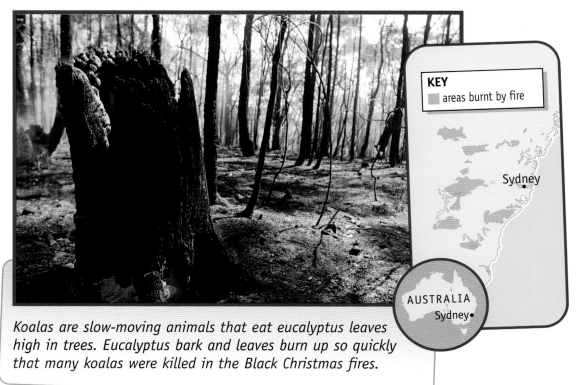

KEY
areas burnt by fire

Sydney

AUSTRALIA
Sydney•

Koalas are slow-moving animals that eat eucalyptus leaves high in trees. Eucalyptus bark and leaves burn up so quickly that many koalas were killed in the Black Christmas fires.

Are forest fires ever useful?

Fire can destroy some **habitats**, and kill **endangered** plants and animals that can never be replaced. However, fires that start naturally, for example after lightning, have always happened in forest and bush lands. Many people believe that such fires cause little or no long-term harm to these wild places, and may even help them.

FIRE FACTS

! Fire can clear away old, dead or dry plants. This reduces the amount of **fuel** that could feed a larger fire in the future.

! Fire turns dead plant parts to **ash** quickly. When it rains, the ash washes into soil, making it good for plants to grow in.

! Fire reduces the number of trees in an area. This allows other trees to grow bigger and new plants to grow in the spaces.

*Some trees actually reproduce during a fire. Lodgepole pine trees grow **cones** that open up and release seeds in the heat of a fire!*

Fire at Yellowstone Park, USA, 1988

In 1988 people were horrified to see towers of flame burning up over half of the famous Yellowstone National Park forest in the Rocky Mountains. Now, **ecologists** have studied the effects of the fire. They have found that although the forest looked ruined, it is recovering quite quickly.

There were patches of unburned ground dotted over the forest. Plants spread quickly from these onto the bare, burned areas. The fire had only burned the top layer of soil, so wildflowers, shrubs and other plants soon sprouted up from seeds and roots below ground. The fire gave them space and allowed more sunlight to reach the new plants.

'Big fires are not bad for the system in any way... for plants and animals, fire is a normal event, well within their capacity to deal with.' Monica Turner, ecologist

CANADA

Yellowstone
National Park

USA

MEXICO

Forests can take many years to recover after a fire, but most will return to their former glory one day. This picture shows new growth of fireweed after a fire.

How do people fight fires?

Forest and bush fires will go on burning as long as they have **fuel**, **oxygen** and heat. **Firefighters** call these three things the 'fire triangle'. To stop a fire they have to remove one or more of the sides of this 'triangle'. This is much harder to do in a forest or bush than it is in a town or city.

Why are forest fires hard to fight?

Firefighters usually put out most city fires within a day. Most buildings contain little wood so city fires do not grow and spread very quickly. Firefighters can get to the fires quickly on city roads. Water and machinery are within easy reach. Forest and bush fires usually start in wild places far from roads and water supplies.

Sometimes the only way to reach forest fires is for helicopters to carry firefighters, equipment and supplies to the heart of the blaze.

Firefighters usually fly over a fire to work out how to deal with it. They ask weather forecasters for advice on which way the wind is blowing. This information helps them work out the direction in which the fires might spread. Weather forecasters also tell firefighters if they can expect any rain, which will help put out the fires.

How do firefighters stop fires spreading?

Some firefighters stop fires by creating a **firebreak**. This is a line of land that has been cleared of plants, trees and leaf litter. A firebreak looks a bit like a narrow track. When a fire reaches a firebreak, it runs out of fuel and so it stops. The firefighters spray water or soil onto the flames until the fire is out.

Workers usually clear firebreaks using tools such as shovels, chainsaws or axes.

How do firefighters reduce the heat?

People use water to put out fires because it absorbs the fire's heat. Forest and bush fires often happen far from water supplies. Fire crews try to get near the fires with their fire engines. Although the engines cannot carry much water, it may be enough to put out a small fire. When fires are large or far from roads, firefighters drop water from helicopters or planes onto the trees and buildings below.

Some engines also carry special foam to spray on homes and buildings. Bubbly foam is a **fire retardant** – it makes buildings less likely to catch alight. Firefighters on land or in the air also sometimes spray chemicals that slow down and cool a fire.

This aeroplane is spraying fire retardant on trees and buildings to slow down the progress of the flames.

Colorado, 2002

On 8 June 2002, a worker in Colorado lit an **illegal** campfire that got out of control. It caused a forest fire, called the Hayman fire, that destroyed 570 square kilometres of forest in just over 3 weeks. That's about as big as a medium-sized city.

Up to 2500 **firefighters** worked to control the Hayman fire, which had flames reaching 100 metres into the air. They used helicopters and aircraft to dump tonnes of water onto hill slopes to soak trees so they would not burn so quickly. Hundreds of homes and other buildings were burned down and 8000 people were **evacuated** with the help of the National Guard.

'This fire burned more acres in one day and burned a greater distance in one day than I've ever seen.' Ron Raley, experienced firefighter

USA

KEY
🔥 Fires

Fort Collins•
Boulder•
🔥Denver
Hayman Fire🔥
•Colorado Springs

COLORADO

Firefighters soaked some areas with water to help keep the flames at bay.

19

What happens after a fire?

When a major fire occurs there are problems that need to be dealt with straight away. There are also problems that take much longer to solve.

Emergency action

One of the first problems is to find places where people can stay when they are **evacuated** from their homes. Some may be able to go to friends' homes further away, but many stay in temporary shelters or in government buildings, like town halls. Often, **aid organizations** supply beds, food and medicines for evacuees. They also supply food and shelter for **firefighters**. Ambulances or helicopters are used to take injured people to hospital. Workers also set up animal holding stations where farm animals or pets are cared for until the fire is out.

Organizations like the Red Cross help people with food and shelter. They also help people find family or friends who have got lost during an evacuation.

Long-term effects

It may be a long time before people can return to their homes. Buildings may need to be rebuilt or made safe. Farmers may lose animals or **crops** in a fire. Sometimes aid organizations send tools and equipment to help people rebuild their businesses.

What happens to land?

Fires can cause serious erosion in forest and bush lands. Erosion is the wearing away of soil and rock. Heat and flames can damage the top layer of soil so badly that water does not drain into it anymore. Rainwater washes over eroded land instead of draining into the soil. This can cause flooding, or landslides, which is when mud and rock slip down the slopes of a hill, damaging houses or people's water supplies.

Shortly after a major fire in Trapper Creek, Idaho, USA in August 1995, heavy rains fell on eroded mountain slopes. Tons of mud and rock washed down the mountain onto a road, washing away this tanker amongst other vehicles.

Can forest fires be predicted?

It is very difficult to predict exactly where and when forest or bush fires will happen. Experts try to work out which areas are at risk of fire and then watch these places carefully for the first signs of smoke.

Fire danger index

Meteorologists are people who study weather conditions. They help predict fires by creating a fire danger index. In the USA, for example, the index starts at 0 and goes up to 100. High numbers indicate a high risk of fire. A fire danger index rating of 100 means fires are extremely likely! Two things that make a fire more likely are drought and high wind speed. Fires are also more likely if there are large amounts of dry plants in an area, which provide **fuel** for a fire.

Some countries have fire seasons – times of the year that are hot and dry, when fires are likely to happen. In North America, extra firefighters are trained for the fire seasons.

Looking back

In some countries, experts try to make very accurate predictions by studying areas where fires have taken place in the past. They look at the weather patterns over previous years and work out how these affected the plants. This information helps them predict when fires will occur in the future.

For example, in California, in the USA, experts discovered that fires are much more likely to happen if two wet winters are followed by a dry winter. The rain in the two wet years encourages lots more plants to grow in forest and **grassland** areas. When these plants dry out in the third winter, they create lots of fuel for fire in the summer months.

It is very difficult to tell where a fire might start. In a dry landscape like this, many fires are started by human carelessness, so it is impossible to predict where they might begin.

Can forest fires be prevented?

'*Only you can prevent forest fires!*' This is the motto of Smokey Bear, a fictional forest **ranger** used by the United States Forest Service to educate people about forest fire safety. People cause many forest blazes, so teaching them to be more careful is one way to prevent fires.

How can I prevent forest or bush fires?

- Find out about the fire rules of an area before you visit it.
- Clear plants and leaf litter away from a campfire before it is lit.
- Throw soil or water on your fire if it gets too big.
- Make sure a campfire is out before you leave it.
- Never use fireworks or drop matches in wild areas.

People should not park their cars on patches of dry grass, because heat from exhaust pipes can start fires.

Smokey Bear, the US Forest Fire Service's most famous ranger!

Fighting fire with fire

Another way of preventing massive forest fires is using **controlled fires**. This is when forest workers burn small fires on wind-free damp days to clear away dead wood, leaf litter and some saplings (very young trees). They also use controlled fires to create **firebreaks**, which are patches of land that are cleared of trees and plants. Fire cannot easily cross a firebreak because there is no **fuel** to burn.

How can people spot fires?

If smaller forest or bush fires can be caught early, people can put them out before they spread. Forest rangers in large forest areas have special high towers. The rangers can see across vast areas and can alert **firefighters** if they spot a fire. In some countries, rangers fly in helicopters to check for signs of danger.

These forest workers are using bulldozers to clear a firebreak in an area of thick forest.

Indonesian forest fires, 1997

The islands of Indonesia are covered with lush **rainforest**. For a long time local people have used **controlled fires** to clear small areas of land to grow food on. The people stop the fires spreading by making **firebreaks**. In the past twenty years, some companies have been burning very big areas of forest to make space for large plantations of oil palm trees. They make money by selling palm oil.

In September 1997, some of these big fires got out of control. They spread because the companies had not made firebreaks, as they wanted the biggest plantations possible. The fires also spread because the trees were very dry after an unusually long time without much rain. In November, rains put out the fires, but they raged again between February and April 1998. The fires burnt almost all the forest areas where people grew food.

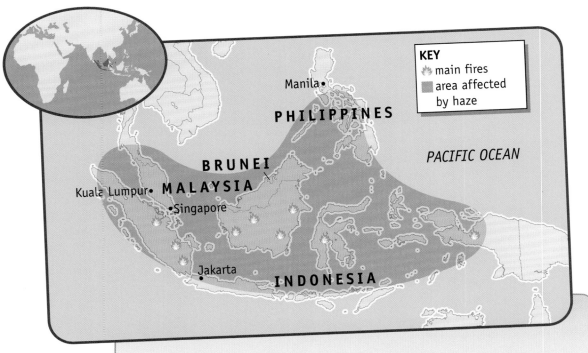

By spring 1998, the fires in Indonesia had affected an area of forest and farmland about as big as the UK.

A dangerous smog

Fire was just part of the danger for people. Autumn winds spread the smoke across five neighbouring countries (see map on page 26). The smoke mixed with air **pollution** and formed a blanket of yellow smog, over countryside and over big cities, such as Singapore. Around 70 million people were affected by breathing problems and eye infections.

Everyday life was affected everywhere. The smoke was so thick in some parts of Indonesia that people could only see a few metres in front of them. Thousands of schools, offices and businesses were closed. Many people were told to stay at home. People were injured in ship and aeroplane collisions.

'This morning, like most mornings, I wake with a headache. In my stomach I feel very strange, and my eyes, they sting. We have not seen the sun for more than a month. We are **suffocating***.'* Zulfan, a taxi driver from Sumatra, Indonesia

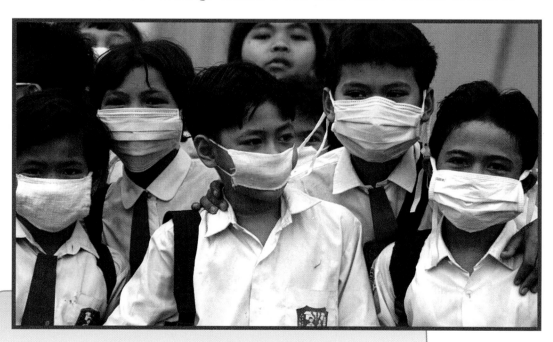

Many people wore facemasks if they went out, to stop them breathing in too much filthy smog.

Will there be forest fires in the future?

A bush or forest fire is an awesome force of nature and people have little control over natural events. Wildfires have always happened and always will. Most are an important part of the cycle of life and growth in a forest or bush land.

People cannot prevent forest fires that start naturally – for example, after lightning strikes a dry patch of grass at the end of a long, hot summer. However, people can prevent many of the fires that start accidentally. Governments can help by carefully controlling companies that cut down trees or alter forests. For example, in Indonesia, the forest fires (see pages 26–27) were largely caused by the activity of palm oil companies. But we can all help by following fire safety rules when we are in forest or bush lands.

*Fires like the 2002 fires in New South Wales, Australia are a fact of life in forests, bush and **grasslands** all over the world – an awesome force of nature that will happen year after year.*

Some major bush and forest fires of the 20th century

1918, Cloquet, Minnesota, USA
Over 400 people died and 5000 square kilometres of trees and the towns of Cloquet and Moose Lake were burned.

1949, Aquitaine, France
A total of 350 fires destroyed 1300 square kilometres of trees.

1982–83, Côte d'Ivoire, West Africa
Wildfires killed over 100 people and burned large areas of land. Coffee, cocoa and other plantations were burned, so many local businesses were ruined.

1983, Ash Wednesday, Australia
Fires killed 75 people and destroyed 2500 houses. In South Australia the loss of sheep, cattle, **pasture** and **crops** was estimated to be worth Aus$5.7 million.

1987, Great Black Dragon Fire, China
Around 73,000 square kilometres of mountainous forest and the homes of 50,000 people were destroyed. Over 200 people died, mostly from smoke fumes.

1988, Yellowstone National Park, USA
In this fire (see page 15) 4000 square kilometres of forest were burned. It cost around US$160 million to fight the fire.

1991, San Francisco, California, USA
Fires raged through residential areas around Oakland, destroying almost 4000 buildings.

1994, New South Wales, Australia
Two-thirds of the Royal National Park were burned, and an estimated 100 species disappeared.

1997, Inner Mongolia
Hundreds of people were killed or injured and over 50,000 people made homeless by nearly 400 fires.

Glossary

aid organizations groups of people that raise money and use it to help others

arson when a fire is lit on purpose to cause damage to people, land or property. It is a crime and the person responsible may go to prison.

ash powdered remains of wood after it is burnt

cone egg-shaped plant part that is made up of lots of overlapping scales. Cones grow on coniferous trees to hold their seeds.

coniferous trees that grow their seeds in cones and have needle-like leaves. They lose and renew leaves all year round, so always look 'evergreen'.

controlled fires fires that are started to clear forest ground. They are kept under control by forestry workers.

crops plants grown by people for food or other uses

ecologists people who study plants, animals and their habitats

ember red hot piece of wood or coal from a fire

endangered plant or animal that is in danger of becoming extinct (dying out)

evacuated (evacuation) when people are moved away from a dangerous place until the danger is over

fire retardant something that stops materials from catching fire

firebreak strip of land cleared of plant life to stop a fire from spreading further

firefighter man or woman who works for the fire service, fighting fires

flammable burns easily

fuel something that can be burned

grassland area of mainly grasses, some shrubs and small trees

habitat natural home of a group of plants and animals

ignite set fire to something

illegal against the law

oxygen gas in the air that animals need to breathe in order to live

pasture areas of grass for farm animals to eat

pollution when part of the environment is poisoned or harmed by human activity

rainforest thick forest in hot places. Rainforests have many tall evergreen trees, ferns and climbing plants.

ranger forest rangers work to protect the trees in a forest and the people who visit

suffocate when someone dies because something, such as smoke fumes, stops them breathing

wilderness wild area where few or no people live

Find out more

Books

Disaster! Fire, Jason Hook (Belitha Press, 2002)

Natural Disasters: Fire and Flood, Nicky Barber (Barron's Educational Series, 1999)

Wildfires, Seymour Simon (Harper Collins, 2000)

World's Worst Fire Disasters, Rob Alcraft and Louise Spilsbury (Heinemann Library, 1996)

Websites

www.howstuffworks.com/wildfire.htm – the How Stuff Works website includes information about how a wildfire is started and spread.

www.fema.gov/kids/wldfire.htm – this site includes useful information about how you can protect your home from a wildfire.

www.smokeybear.com – this is the website of Smokey Bear, the US Forest Fire Service's most famous bear!

Disclaimer
All the Internet addresses (URLs) given in this book were valid at the time of going to press. However, due to the dynamic nature of the Internet, some addresses may have changed, or sites may have changed or ceased to exist since publication. While the author and publishers regret any inconvenience this may cause readers, no responsibility for any such changes can be accepted by either the author or the publishers.

Index